Be Your Own Boss

Alison Stokes

ACCENT PRESS LTD

INTRODUCTION

Have you ever dreamed of being your own boss? Maybe, while waiting for the bus to work or scanning the adverts in the Jobcentre window, you've thought how much happier you would be if you were in control. Just think, if you ran your own business, you would never have to face rejection of your job applications, or the daily fear of a grumpy boss, or the unhappiness of not making the grade in your exams. You could be in charge of your own career destiny.

Entrepreneurs are all around us: they're on TV in programmes like *Dragon's Den* or *The Secret Millionaire*. The name may conjure up images of high-flying businesspeople like Sir Alan Sugar or Deborah Meaden, but it's just another word for people who have bright ideas and the can-do attitude to turn those ideas into money-making ventures. They are not a super species born to be rich. In all walks of life, from café owners or mechanics to eBayers, there are ordinary people who have turned their ideas or talent into a way to earn a living.

Anything is possible. All you need is an idea and a plan. That idea could be a clever invention, a solution to a common problem, a home-made product that people want to buy, or a skill that someone else will pay for. Whether you clean cars, drive taxis, cut lawns, bake cakes, sell clothes or build houses, if enough people are prepared to pay you – you could have your own enterprise.

Every week almost 150 new businesses start up in Wales. And the good news is – you're never too old, or too young. Recent figures show there has been a rise in the number of over-fifties who have decided to become self-employed after losing their jobs. These are people who have worked for someone else for most of their life but are not happy on the dole. At the opposite end of the age scale, as youth unemployment remains high, many young people are choosing to work for themselves. Currently, one in twenty young people are self-employed and that number is expected to increase to one in five in the next five years. They want to break free from the depressing cycle of 'no job, no experience: no experience, no job'.

As you read on you'll uncover start-up stories from people all over Wales. Chapter by chapter, these unexpected entrepreneurs will explain the basics of what you need to get started. There are tips on how to launch your idea with little or no money, and advice on where you can go for grants to help you start out. These stories aim to fire up your imagination and your drive to better yourself.

So are you ready to *Be Your Own Boss*?

Chapter One

THE BIG IDEA

Most new businesses start with that 'light bulb moment' – a sudden flash of inspiration. Some entrepreneurs may already be working in their specialised field when they spot a gap in the market for their new business idea, while others may see ways of improving an existing product. You might look at your own working history and see how you could offer a better or different service. What about the times when you've needed a particular service or product and realised there's no one out there doing it? If you need it, is there a chance that others will too?

The big idea is just the starting point on your journey. Your friends and family might laugh at your ideas, but don't let that put you off. When Richard Pring told his friends he was making a mobile phone app based around a cute, furry ginger kitten that could do sums, they bet him it wouldn't work.

Within a year more than 100,000 mobile phone and tablet owners around the world had downloaded the Kitten Calculator. It was the start of success for Richard's new games and app development company, Wales Interactive Ltd.

'It started out as a bet with a friend who said my app would never sell,' explains Richard, who studied for a degree in computer programming and animation at the University of Glamorgan. 'So I wanted to prove him wrong and I was right. Every day someone, somewhere in the world, is downloading a Kitten Calculator.'

The idea to launch Wales's first dedicated computer games and app development company came to Richard and his partner, Dai Banner, after they had spent two years working together on a project called the Games Lab. Based at the University of Glamorgan's Atrium campus, the Games Lab was a scheme funded by the Welsh Government which revived the games industry in Wales. At the time there were computer programmers dotted around Wales working away on their own but no one seemed to be talking to one another. Richard and Dai helped to bring those game designers together to share and develop their ideas. When the project ended they realised there was a gap in the market and decided to set up their own business. Richard had the technical background, while Dai had sixteen years of experience in the international games industry. He had worked for the London company that launched the very first Tomb Raider game.

They launched their own company in July 2012, with just two staff working in offices in the former Sony factory near Bridgend. Within the first twelve months the partners had employed eighteen new games creators and animators. In that time they released fifteen new games and apps. These included their first ever game on PlayStation 3 – Reboot. They even beat the BBC's *Doctor Who* games to win a BAFTA Cymru Award for their app game Candy the Magic Dinosaur.

'Initially we started out as an independent games developer which meant we could take more risks, with small teams just making stuff we liked. But we did much better than we expected,' says Richard.

'I thought I knew a bit about business but within the first year I realised how little I knew. So I signed up on a business start-up course with Business in Focus and my advisor was really useful and had lots of advice to help with things I hadn't foreseen.'

In addition to creating their own games for

mobile phones, tablets, PCs and the main games consoles, the company has also been able to use its experience to help smaller app developers launch their creations on iTunes and Android. It is also working on launching the first Welsh-language game on PlayStation 3.

'We started out with targets for our first year and we did much better than we expected. It was a crazy year. The PlayStation project took us eight months to develop but that is a real skill we can use to build on. Our worst-case scenario for the first year was that me and Dai would end up sitting in a room working on our own but in the event we've sustained a much bigger team than we expected.

'The app market has grown so much that it is getting saturated and you just don't know how well a game is going to do. The chance of making millions from one app is like winning a lottery ticket – it's hard to do, but the more experience you get, the more you know exactly what you're doing and that's where we have an advantage.'

Richard's top tip

Never be afraid to ask questions even if it means sounding stupid.

Sports masseur Lisa Edwards got her business idea from a work placement. Working behind the checkout at her local Spar store in Rhyl was not her ideal job!

Luckily for Lisa, she had carried out a student work placement at her local football club, Rhyl FC, while she was studying for a degree in sports therapy. That led to the club offering her a part-time job as the club's physiotherapist. For two evenings a week it was her role to be on the side of the pitch to treat any players and strap up their injuries during matches. Off the pitch she could help them with exercises and therapy to restore them to full fitness. And that's what gave her the idea to start out on her own as a sports therapist.

Lisa explains: 'Although I was working at the football club, I was having difficulty finding a full-time job in sports therapy because I didn't have enough experience. I had a job working at Spar but it wasn't what I wanted to do. That's when I thought that maybe I could work for myself.

'There was a physiotherapy room at the football club that was not being used to its full potential. It had a therapy table but it needed a bit of TLC. So I approached the club managers and asked how they would feel about me running my own business from the club. They agreed and it all started from there.'

'I carried out research to see what competition was in the area. I identified three or four local therapists and rang to find out how much they charged. Some of them were well established and had more than twenty years' experience, so I decided to set my prices a bit lower because I was just starting out. The Prince's Trust gave me help to develop my idea and also gave me a £700 grant to set up. With that money I set about redecorating the physio room at the football club and bought new towels and furniture to make it look nice.'

In 2011 L. E. Sports Therapy opened for business. 'The first couple of months were really slow but after that it started to build up. I put posters around the football club to advertise what I was doing and went around the area putting leaflets through letter boxes, but that didn't really work. My first customers were people I already knew.

'During my first year I went on courses to keep my knowledge up to date. I also found that more than half of my clients were not sporty people, they were just ordinary people with back problems or pulled muscles, so I extended my services to offer a wider variety of treatment for people who had had car accidents and for older people to restore mobility.'

As her business grew Lisa moved from the football club to open a new clinic in Rhyl's High Street and found work with other football clubs in the area. She also secured new contracts to deliver physiotherapy services for people off work with injuries, and chair exercises for elderly care-home residents.

'Sometimes working for yourself can be hard. Mostly I run my own day, but sometimes the day runs me. I have quiet weeks and I get really busy weeks. When it's quiet I go looking for more business. It's never so quiet that I have nothing to do. I like the flexibility of working for myself.'

Lisa's top tip

Don't do anything for free – you have to make a living.

Chapter Two

ENJOY WHAT YOU DO

If you can base your business around something that makes you happy, and can make a profit, then you are more likely to succeed. Lorry driver Rob Eley found his big idea while rummaging around the contents of a dead person's house!

At school Rob hated reading and writing, but that didn't stop him from setting up his own business. 'When I was younger I struggled to read big words. Whenever the teachers made me read out loud in front of the class, I would make mistakes and everyone would laugh at me. It put me off reading for life.' In addition to his poor reading, Rob also found it hard to concentrate in the classroom. 'I was always forgetting things and I had a hard time passing my GCSEs,' he admits. 'I liked science and my maths wasn't too bad. I got through my exams, but I only had a D in English. I didn't want to go to college. Anyway my mother couldn't afford to send me to college, so as soon as I left school I had to get a job.'

A week after leaving school, Rob was lucky to find a job at a local factory in Port Talbot, where his uncle worked. For two years he worked there making glass units for windows and doors. But then he wanted a change. He first tried working in telephone sales, and over the years drifted into a variety of jobs in factories, and even worked as a bouncer in nightclubs around Swansea and Port Talbot for a while. But he wanted a job that gave him more security and so started work at a bakery, driving a lorry delivering their fresh bread to supermarkets every day.

'I would get up at midnight to be at the factory by 1 a.m. to collect the bread. Then I'd deliver it to the supermarkets. By 10 a.m. my shift would be over and I would be going home to bed while everyone else was getting up for work. It was really tough. I couldn't get into a routine where I could sleep in the day. So I was walking around like a zombie most of the time. I enjoyed the driving part of my job; I just didn't like the hours.'

As the recession hit, the bakery started making job cuts and Rob moved from one haulage company to another. 'I would be in a job but as soon as work went quiet I would get sacked. I was fed up with the situation. I worked so hard but no one seemed to appreciate it. I was told to sign up for jobs with job agencies. I registered with a few and waited around. But I never heard anything from them. So I decided enough was enough and I would set up my own company, though I wasn't sure what I would do.'

Then one day, a friend asked Rob to help him out. His uncle, who lived in England, had passed away and the friend and his mum had to clear his house. They needed someone to hire a van and drive across the country to help with the removals.

'It sounds a bit weird, but even though it was a sad time, I enjoyed doing it,' says Rob. 'I watched the reality TV programme *Storage Wars*. I was fascinated how the auctioneers on the programme would clear the contents of storage lockers and sell them off for profit. It made me think it might be something I could do for a living.'

With that idea in his mind, Rob approached the Prince's Trust charity who sent him on a course which helped him draw up a plan of action for his business. He was also given help to apply for grants for equipment and building his company website. Spending the small savings he had put aside as a deposit to buy a house, Rob bought a second-hand van. With a vehicle of his own, he then spent the next few months building up customers and developing a good reputation for his work. In April 2013 at the age of twenty-nine, he launched Eley's Removals & Clearances. Covering his home town of Port Talbot and the surrounding areas, Rob started advertising his services as a 'man with a van' available for house, garden and building clearances, and home and office removals. He also extended his services into property cleaning on behalf of landlords and estate agents.

'When I started out on the course I was told not to expect to make money for the first three years. But I started making money instantly. I found a couple of bidding sites on the internet, where I could register and bid for work. Starting at the bottom, I had to cut my prices to get the jobs. But the more work I did, the more I built my reputation and could charge more.

'House clearance work is not for everyone. I've seen some disgusting things. Once I was asked to do a job for an estate agent. The tenants had been kicked out of a house and I had to go in and clean it up. The house was filthy. In one of the bedrooms there was a pile of human teeth. It was horrible. I had to completely strip the house. Take the carpets out and everything. I couldn't believe the people who had been living there had brought their children up in such a disgusting place. It was not my favourite job.

'Working for yourself can be hard at the start. I would work seven days a week. During the summer months I was working from 7 a.m. to 10 p.m. on house and garden clearances. Then I went through a quiet patch, and started to worry that I had made the wrong choice. But just when I began to think that I would not get any more work, business picked up and I realised that working for myself was definitely the right decision.'

Rob's top tip

If there's something you've always wanted to do – give it a go.

Listening to rap and reggae music made teenager Nathan Dicks happy. Studying for exams did not. And it was his love of music and song words that gave him his big idea to revolutionise the way teenagers and young adults learn.

'Throughout school I was always in the lower classes. I was a D to C grade student,' explains Nathan. 'My spelling and writing were appalling and my literacy was poor. I was suffering from dyslexia, although I didn't know it at the time. My teachers were always shouting at me for getting things wrong. And I would get into trouble with some of them. I felt that they thought I was stupid, and I wanted to prove them wrong.'

One day, as he was sitting in his bedroom listening to the radio rather than focusing on his GCSE English studies, a rap song caught his interest. 'Without realising it, I sang along to all the words to "Changes" by Tupac. And that's when a light bulb went on in my head. I said to myself: "What if all the characters and plot from the Shakespeare play I was studying were lyrics in a rap song? There would be no reason why I wouldn't take that in subconsciously, like I had with Tupac's lyrics. It could break down the barrier of picking up books."

'I was well into reggae and hip-hop music. Artists like Bob Marley, Peter Tosh and Dennis Brown told stories that empowered the listener.

They had an attitude that was all about being positive. So when teachers were telling me I couldn't do things, I would take a lesson from music and think, "I'll prove you wrong." '

Ignoring his careers teacher's advice to try for an apprenticeship at the local steelworks, Nathan left school and found work at a large office near Cardiff. It was his job to type information into computers all day, every day. 'One day my work-mates in the office were complaining about the way things were done. I volunteered to go and talk to the boss. I knocked on his office door and went in. I explained how a group of us workers had thought of a way that we could work faster. "I pay you to type, not think," he said. It stuck in my mind and I was determined that one day I would work for myself.'

It would be another four years before Nathan took the brave step to launch his own business. In the meantime he was accepted to study applied economics at Swansea University. 'On my first day at university I walked into my student flat and my flat-mate asked if I liked music. It turned out he loved reggae too. For the first two weeks we sat in the kitchen listening to music. We talked about how we would change the world, make loads of money and give it away. At the end of the year we decided to stop talking and do something. So we came up with the idea for a student magazine.'

However, the friends had no money to put their ideas into practice. But then, the owner of a local music club, where his friend worked part-time, offered them free use of the club on a quiet Sunday night to put on a fund-raising event. They had just a week to organise everything: hire bands to play, design flyers and hand them out to friends and students to promote it. To their surprise hundreds of people turned up. 'At the end of the night we counted up the money and we had a couple of thousand pounds. We thought: screw the magazine, let's keep doing this.'

Starting an events company, Nathan and his friend spent the next two years putting all their time and effort into organising reggae music nights in clubs around Swansea. As his reputation grew, Nathan found himself DJ-ing at events all over the country, sometimes alongside reggae heroes. 'I couldn't believe how we had gone from being in the kitchen talking about music, to actually making money for doing something we loved. Working as a DJ in clubs made me realise how special music was. I would watch people who would normally be fighting on the streets, but who, inside the club with the music playing, were talking and dancing together. It convinced me that music had a special power over young people.'

In 2008, he left university with a degree and a diagnosis that he suffered from dyslexia, and took the decision to help teenagers like himself learn through music. From his bedroom in Swansea, he set up Rewise Learning. Its aim was to create unique teaching programmes for schools and pupils aged 14–16 years old. Transforming English, science and maths lessons into raps and pop songs, the Learn Thru Music programme was born.

For the first year it was tough. Business was slow and he lost money. But Nathan's fortunes changed with an invitation to meet the Prime Minister.

'The Prince's Trust charity, which had given me a loan when I started out, was invited to a conference in Cardiff with Prime Minister Gordon Brown and they asked me and some other young entrepreneurs to go along. At first I was reluctant. National newspaper journalists and TV cameras were going to be there and they wanted young people to ask the Prime Minister questions. I had never spoken in public and didn't think I would be able to stand up in front of so many important people. When the time came, I was really nervous. Someone on the stage asked if anyone had a question for the Prime Minister. I felt like I couldn't do it. The voice in my head was saying, "You can't do it." But I raised my hand in the air and they picked me. I stood up.

'I didn't actually have a question but there was a sign behind Gordon Brown which said "Make Britain's Future Better". I said, "Good morning, Prime Minister, I'm here to help you make Britain's future better." As you can imagine, everyone in the room turned to look at me. The Prime Minister was shocked and asked me how I intended to do that. So I explained all about my idea for learning through music. I said to him, "I bet you can remember all the words of your favourite songs when you were fourteen. Well, that's what I want to do to help young people learn." I made him promise to help me. He gave me his business card with his address, 10 Downing Street, London, and promised he would help me roll the programme out across the UK. I couldn't believe my luck. Suddenly I was the centre of attention. All the press in the room wanted to interview me about my ideas. I was on news channels all over the world.'

The sudden exposure gave Nathan's business the boost it needed. He was put onto a national learning programme register and was given the help he needed to licence his learning programme with local councils. It was the start of Nathan's business success. Over the following years more than 20,000 young people and adults have used Rewise Learning's unique music programme, which turns important facts in Key Stage 4 science, maths and English lessons into song lyrics. His programme is used in schools in Wales and England. He has been invited to dinner with Prince Charles, patron of the Prince's Trust charity, and visited America with other young entrepreneurs. He also runs courses through the Prince's Trust, where he helps disadvantaged young people learn literacy and numeracy through music. Learn Thru Music is also developing a new interactive website where its songs can be downloaded for modern students. 'When we are young we learn our times tables through music and we learn nursery rhymes which stick in our heads for life.

What I do is no different. Who says that when you get older you have to stop having fun when learning?

'If you get on a crazy path to running your own business, wonderful things can happen. It's all part of the journey. When I was a teenager, sitting in my bedroom struggling with my exams, I never dreamed I would be travelling the world and meeting famous people. I just wanted to help kids learn with music. But if it can happen to me it can happen to anyone. You just have to be prepared to take a chance and work hard.'

Nathan's top tip:

Grab opportunities when you can.

Chapter Three

TURN YOUR PASSION INTO PROFIT

Surfer Ben Room first had the idea that he could turn his passion for skateboarding, surfing and snowboarding into a business while working as an instructor on the Gower.

As a teenager he was never good at academic subjects, scraping by with two Ds and an E at A level, but he had always been keen on board sports. By the age of nineteen he had dropped out of college twice and, with no plans to go to university, he decided to take a year out working in Australia. 'I was offered a job in Australia but soon afterwards I had a motorbike accident and couldn't go,' explains Ben. 'It took me six months to recover from the injuries and I didn't know what I would do next.'

While recovering he discovered a course in water and adventure sports management, which was being run at Swansea Institute. That appealed to his sporting interests, so he applied and was offered a place the following year. During the course Ben spent six months of the year studying, then six months on work placements. In the first year he worked at a water sports centre in Greece. The following year he jetted off to an island in the Caribbean.

However, as he started his third year, Ben's girlfriend announced she was expecting a baby. When their daughter was born his focus changed. With the extra responsibility of a family to support, Ben contacted a surf school close to his home on the Gower for his final placement. He made such a good impression during his six-month placement, they offered him a job.

'One day during the school summer holidays we had a group of 15–16 year-old lads from a community group in the Valleys who came down to the Gower for surf lessons. When they arrived the minibus driver took me to one side and warned me about one of the boys who had been causing trouble on the journey. Driving through the village, this lad had opened the fire exit on the bus and shouted, "You surfer bums, get a job," to the local surfers. I decided I needed to take a military approach with them. I started by giving them lots of press-ups to do and told them horror stories about how dangerous the beach could be. When I took them down to the sea with their surfboards, the boy in question was a classic case of overconfidence. He was trying too hard, jumping onto the board too quickly and falling off. I took him to one side, away from the group, and taught him how to stand on the board. By the end of the day, I got him surfing. When the session was over and all the other boys had gone into the showers, the boy tapped me on the shoulder and asked, "Ben, where can I get one of these boards?" Driving home, I felt good that in one afternoon I had changed this boy's idea of surfers. But then I started to think that it was unlikely that the lad would carry on surfing if his family didn't have money to spend on buying him surfing equipment or for driving fifty miles or so to a beach.

'That got me thinking about a mountainboarding centre as a way of taking surfing to kids in the Valleys, showing them what useful natural terrain they had around them. With skateboarding you have to wait for the weather, with surfing you wait for the waves, and with kiteboarding you wait for the wind, but mountainboarding isn't affected by the Welsh weather.'

Quitting his job at the surf school, Ben spent

two months job-hunting and thinking about his boarding business idea. For the first year he worked on developing and marketing his business idea, while working shifts as a lifeguard and swimming teacher. He drove around farms in the area searching for an empty field to launch his business. Eventually he found a sloping field at Weobley Castle, knocked on the farmer's door and asked permission to use it. Initially the farmer allowed him free use of the land in exchange for customers visiting his farm shop. Eventually Ben found support from the business school at Swansea University which helped him secure a grant and interest-free loan. With the money in place he bought twenty-five mountainboards, helmets, knee, elbow and wrist pads, and launched BRD Sports in 2008.

As the business developed, the recession hit and Ben found his customers changing. Stag party groups, birthday parties and groups of work colleague on team-building days out were still booking, but with the cost of petrol rising, fewer individuals were prepared to travel to the Gower for sessions. In addition to this he had started paying rent to the farmer for the use of the field, so he needed to increase his turnover. To meet the challenge, Ben returned to his initial idea of offering his mountainboarding to groups in deprived areas.

In 2010 he was presented with an award for a project. 'That made me realise that I wanted to concentrate my business more on social enterprises where we would put profits back into developing the sport. One of our regular riders won first place in the National Championships in 2012, so I want to look at ways to raise money to build a new block of showers and changing rooms at the centre. That way we can run international competitions in the future. I've also been working with charities in the Valleys to help them get funding to buy their own boards. That way we can provide young people with board proficiency and safety training, so they can go boarding where they live. Working with disadvantaged groups is at the heart of where I saw the business when I started out.'

Ben's top tip

Make sure you file your accounts on time. In my first year I was fined £400 for missing a deadline.

Chapter Four

NO IDEAS, NO WORRIES

Not everyone can be bursting with ideas and creativity, but there are other ways of getting started. A popular option is franchising. This is where you enter an agreement and pay a fee for a licence with an already established and successful business (the franchisor) that allows you to trade under their brand name. There are franchises in everything, from children's nurseries to garden maintenance, accountants to estate agents, coffee shops to Chinese takeaways. Well-known names such as Burger King, McDonald's, Dyno-Rod, Clarks shoes, Cash Generator and AutoGlym offer this type of opportunity. And if you do your homework and find the right one to suit you, it can be an easier way to find a ready-made customer base.

Cardiff driving instructor Keith Willicombe did just that. He started working for himself by taking out a franchise with an already-established driving school in his area. Now he charges other driving instructors a fee to trade under his own popular Bumps driving-school name.

After being made redundant from his job for the second time in almost ten years, Keith vowed he was going to do something about it. 'I said to myself I never again wanted to be in the position of facing the devastation of losing my job and worrying how I was going to pay my mortgage,' he recalls. So he decided to spend £3,500 on retraining to become a driving instructor. It was a gamble. Three out of ten people who took the course failed. There was also a lot of competition from the 800 other instructors on the roads of Cardiff. 'I had no clients of my own, no car and not a lot of money. I didn't know where to advertise or how successful that would be. As I was still learning my trade, it was difficult to know where to start.' He felt that the best option would be to take out a franchise with a well-established driving school. By paying £210 a week he was provided with a car and a regular stream of pupils who wanted to learn to drive. 'It was a good starting point. From the clients the driving school provided I was taking enough money to pay the franchise fee every month and make a reasonable profit on top of that.'

But two years later Keith realised that he had built up enough clients of his own and he could save more than half his monthly bills if he leased his own car and started his own business. In April 2005 Keith took the risk to strike out on his own. He bought three new Ford Fiestas from his local garage and hired a newly qualified female instructor to join him on the road. For the first eight months business ticked over slowly by word of mouth.

But at the end of 2005, his luck changed.

'I took a gamble and spent £5,500 on a half-page advertisement in the Yellow Pages. That Christmas it seemed that everyone had money and when January came, my phone didn't stop ringing. Every ten minutes, when I was in the middle of a lesson, I was getting calls from people wanting to book lessons with us. I had sixty-two new pupils in the first month, then continued to grow at a rate of thirty-three new customers a month after that. I needed to take on more instructors and had to come up with my own idea for a franchise which I called Bumps Drivin's Cool, as a play on the traditional words "driving school".'

Knowing how much the other driving schools charged, Keith set his prices lower and offered newer cars to his instructors. Soon the word spread around Cardiff. For the next eighteen months Keith was able to recruit a new instructor every month, many moving from his competitors. The following year Keith spent more on advertising and it worked. Soon he had twenty-three instructors working under the Bumps name. And at one point the company was turning over more than £600,000 a year. But as the driving school grew, so did the cost of maintaining the cars. Some months his bill for new tyres alone would be more than £700. 'It was getting to be a real headache. Then I had the bright idea of changing the franchise. I would reduce the fees I was charging the instructors, they would have to supply their own cars and I would act as a booking agent for their new customers. It relieved the burden of running a fleet of cars. The franchise option continued to work until the recession hit; competition became more fierce as rival driving schools started reducing their hourly rates for lessons. Some of Keith's instructors left to find other work. But Bumps has continued its success. 'My early success was meteoric, but it was a learning curve,' says Keith. 'I still get enquiries from driving instructors wanting to take out a franchise but I am happy with the level of business we have and I'm not looking to expand. I would rather keep the instructors I have with a decent number of pupils each week rather than take on more cars.

'I was lucky I started out when I did. I took the gamble of advertising in the Yellow Pages and it worked. Putting all your advertising into one place wouldn't work today as people don't use the Yellow Pages as much and there are so many search engines and companies offering to increase Google rankings that it's trial and error knowing what will work. Fortunately, the name Bumps is now established and we trade off our name and recommendations. I still spend £20,000 a year in advertising and the instructors who take out a franchise would rather be part of an established company than try to survive on their own, so it works for everyone.'

Keith's top tip

Making money from a franchise is hard work and requires a long-term financial and personal commitment.

Chapter Five

THE PLAN

So you've got your big idea, and you know what you want to do to make your fortune. Now comes the sensible stuff: the Business Plan. So what is a Business Plan and why is it important?

Basically, it's taking all those ideas floating around in your head and putting them down on paper in a way that others can understand. It's really important if you're hoping to get funding or borrow money to get your idea off the ground. It's also really helpful to highlight any possible problems before they happen.

A good business plan will explain your idea in a simple yet interesting way. If writing plans is not your strong point, there are plenty of experts out there who can help. Go to any of the websites or organisations listed in the final chapter – there are templates to follow and advisors on hand to guide you through. It will be worth it in the end.

Former railway worker Brian Hancock found out the importance of having a plan when he set out to run his own self-defence classes in Carmarthenshire. He needed £4,000 to buy mats and a trailer to transport them. But when he went to his bank to ask for money, the manager just laughed. In his head Brian knew how he wanted to run a series of self-defence classes, but on paper he had nothing. 'The bank manager treated me as if it was some sort of joke,' Brian recalls. 'It was disheartening but I went to my mortgage company and got an extra loan on my mortgage and launched Harmony Health and Defence.'

Brian didn't consider himself a businessman: for twenty-one years he had worked in a full-time job and in his spare time trained in the Japanese martial art of aikido. But in 2003 he suffered a knee injury and mental health problems and was made redundant from his job at the Llanelli signal box on medical grounds. 'I was forty-two and had worked on the railways for most of my life. When I lost my job I was caring for my wife and needed to find work that could fit around my commitments. One day my aikido teacher (or sensei) said, "You'd make a good teacher, why don't you start your own self-defence classes?" '

Brian first found his interest in martial arts in 1989 when his son was being bullied at school and he took him along to an aikido class. 'As I sat watching my son training, I thought it looked easy and joined in. At first I was terrible. I thought I could look after myself, but an 11-year-old girl threw me on my backside ten times and I had no idea how she did it. She seemed to use no strength at all and yet I couldn't beat her. I wanted to know how she did it.' Starting off at beginner's level, Brian trained hard and worked his way up to the highest fifth grade, or black belt. When his Sensei gave him the idea to start his own classes Brian was on benefits, so he went to the Jobcentre and they put him on to the Enterprise Allowance Scheme, which paid benefits for the first six months while he was setting up and helped with mentoring and advice.

'At first, the plan was to hire a school in the area and advertise locally. I borrowed some old mats from my sensei; they were a bit tatty but didn't cost me anything. I had 2,000 leaflets printed and, with some help from my son and daughter, I spent a week walking the streets posting them through letter boxes and sticking them in shop windows and on notice boards.

On the first night only five women turned up. I had spent £100 on hiring the hall and the five customers paid £25 each for a two-day course, so I didn't lose money. But I realised that all the effort I had put in with posters and leaflets wasn't the right way to market myself. I didn't think that having a male instructor might put women off, I just wanted to teach people.

'The next plan was to put posters up and advertise in local newspapers and radio stations and write letters to schools. I didn't know much about emails and couldn't use a computer. So I wrote hundreds of letters by hand and sent them to the heads of schools in the county. I had hardly any response to begin with.'

Eventually Brian contacted a local business advice centre, which gave him help to draw up a business plan and arranged a reduced rate for him to advertise in his local newspaper. 'After that, work started to pick up. By the second year I was getting regular business. Each month I opened my bank statement and I had enough money to pay the bills, and for me that was a success.

'I found that once I had a business plan I could get more help with finance for my business. The plan showed that the business could work. Once I was able to show that I was trying, there were people willing to help. As soon as I had my plan in place I was able to get a £1,000 grant from a "Menter a Busnes" scheme which helped me buy a computer and paid a company to create my website. I also had a grant to advertise my company on Swansea Sound radio.'

Then a friend suggested Brian should get in touch with the Prince's Trust, who hired him to run classes in Pembroke for young people on their young offenders programme. The course was a success and it gave him the idea of focusing his teaching efforts on young people and schools. Around the same time Brian had a call from a woman who ran an after-school club in Llandeilo. She had heard about Brian's classes through her colleagues in other schools and wanted him to run sessions at her club. Gradually, as the word spread about the success of his classes and demonstrations, Brian was able to offer more schools sessions aimed at low achievers who didn't fit in with the National Curriculum. Harmony Health and Defence classes offered students an alternative to academic lessons. Brian explains: 'We were giving them something to motivate them and teach them how to have a positive attitude. There is no anger or aggression in our school classes, we just teach them to be positive and we have a high success rate in developing pupils' interest in martial arts.' Now school classes make up the main business for Brian's Harmony Health and Defence, and offer everything from demonstrations for Japanese-themed days to alternative curriculum classes.

In 2008 Brian's health problems returned and he considered closing his business, rather than letting customers and students down. However, fate stepped in when his daughter Heidi was made redundant from her factory job in Llanelli. She shared her father's passion for aikido and offered to help him out. Not only did she take over her father's classes, she expanded the business. With a woman in charge, the female self-defence classes became a hit. She developed links with the charity Women's Aid, setting up courses for victims of domestic abuse, as well as teaching nurses and hospital staff and women hotel workers. In addition to martial arts, the company has also been able to specialise in character-building and relaxation classes.

'Heidi has really taken to the business. She has been practising aikido since she was eight and used to train with the adults, so I was happy to pass the business on to her. Now I help her when my health allows me,' explains Brian.

'My only regret is that I didn't get more advice when I was first starting up. Being a typical man I thought I knew what I was doing. If I had been more open to help I probably could have had grants from the Welsh Government to buy new mats right at the beginning rather than borrowing money against my house. There is plenty of help available if you know where to look.'

Brian's top tip

Go for it. And when you hit a pitfall, keep pushing yourself. If you fail, at least you've tried.

Chapter Six

START SMALL, KEEP YOUR COSTS DOWN

Once you have your idea and have drawn up your plan, you will need to consider where you are going to operate. Consider working from home. With a good internet connection and a computer many businesses can be run from home, which helps to keep the costs down as you start to build your business. Popular home business ideas include child care, tutoring, translation, web design, catering, art and craft making, publishing, consultancy, therapy, editorial services, dog walking and alteration services.

Animal lover Michelle Inch, aged twenty-five, who runs the upmarket Pawfection Pet Boutique in Barry, is a great example of how a virtual shop can become a real one. She started out grooming dogs from her parents' home in Barry as a teenager. Then, after taking time out to be a mum, she wanted to get back into the pet pampering business.

Michelle spent thousands of pounds a year on treats for her own pet horses and her two dogs, a Tea-cup Chihuahua named Peekaboo and Fernando the poodle, and realised there were other pet owners who also liked to make their animals feel special. So she started making dog and pony jewellery from her home in Barry, which she sold on eBay.

'I have always treated my pets as part of my family and felt they deserved to be spoilt and pampered now and then. I started out by making a few ranges of my own products – dog necklaces made from crystals and pearls, blingy bow ties and crystal horse bridles and plaiting braids for dressage horses. I also sold dog clothes, which I bought from other makers, and sold on through my online shop. By selling online my overheads were low. I only paid the fees for listing the items and selling them. I didn't really advertise my products, yet they sold well with people who were looking for accessories for their pets. Some members of the cast of *The Only Way is Essex* bought some of the collars I was selling, so I thought I must be on the right track. It confirmed what I had already thought, that there were a lot of potential customers out there who treated their pets like their own children.'

In 2011 Michelle approached the Prince's Trust with a plan to set up a pet boutique with a grooming parlour in the back. She says, 'Other businesses in the area thought I was crazy opening in the current climate, but I felt that the time was right for the products and services I was planning to sell.'

Raising £40,000 in loans from her parents and the Prince's Trust, Michelle searched for a property in the right location for her business. 'I would have loved to open in Cowbridge but the rent in Barry was cheaper,' she explains. 'I chose the location in Park Road as it is close to Porthkerry Park and a lot of dog walkers pass every day on their way to the park.' Michelle and her partner, who is a builder, worked long hours converting the empty shop into a plush pampering salon with a diamanté chandelier, polished granite flooring, and plush French furniture.

As well as the usual grooming, Michelle's pet spa has a luxury walk-in wetroom. She offers doggy facials to remove tear stains, pet fur dyes and glitter treatments costing up to £100. She even has a range of glittery nail paint manicures and brightly coloured claw caps for dogs. Her boutique sells dog clothing and shoes, customised collars and leads, quirky fancy dress costumes, and her own hand-made dog necklaces. Customers can also buy specialised dog food, dog ice cream and birthday cakes. Within months of opening Michelle had built up more than 2,000 clients. Her customers included local celebrities and Premier League footballers' wives and girlfriends (WAGs, as they're known). She also made newspaper headlines all over Britain with pooch pampering sessions and was even invited on to Alan Titchmarsh's TV chat show to discuss the health benefits of her pampering products.

'At first some people were concerned that using nail varnish was bad for the animals, but I've done my research and the products I use are water-based and are non-toxic like children's nail varnishes. The claw caps look like fake nails for dogs. They are bright and fun but they also protect your household floors from being scratched. And the facial helps to remove tear stains from a dog's face, particularly dogs with light-coloured fur. I am also developing my own range of holistic pet therapy products like paw massage bars for dogs, glitter hoof oil for horses, and shampoos. I have to work with laboratories to test them for safety.'

In 2013 Michelle was named a Young Ambassador for the Prince's Trust in 2013 to inspire other young entrepreneurs. She says: 'People said I was mad to open a dog boutique but it only spurred me on to prove them wrong. I run the dog grooming business to pay the bills and the boutique side of the business for profit.'

Michelle's top tip

Selling your new products online doesn't cost a lot of money and is a great way to find out if anyone wants to buy them.

Chapter Seven

HOW TO MAKE MONEY FROM A HOBBY

Ask yourself: what do you enjoy doing in your spare time, and can you make money from it? Maybe you make your own beer, which goes down well with friends and family. Perhaps you sew clothes for your children, which are the envy of other mums at the school gates. Could you turn your interest into an enterprise? This is what is known as a 'hobby' business, where you take something you enjoy doing and sell the product or service to other people. For many people this can be a good way to work from home or test the water with their ideas and products without giving up their day job. There's a growing trend of 'five-to-niners': people who are employed by day but spend their evenings running their own business. It's also something that works well for parents wanting to earn a little extra cash in what is called a 'pocket-money' business.

Cardiff mums Liz Salter and Allison Morgan came up with their idea for their own cupcake baking business, Dotty Cupcakes, three years ago when their youngest children were at primary school. At every school fête and fundraising event, the two friends always seemed to end up behind the cake stall.

'My husband worked away from home a lot and my children were at school all day, so I wanted to do something that would make a bit of extra money and that I could fit around my family,' explains Liz. 'I'd always been interested in baking. My father was a chef and his family used to run a bakery in Cardiff for more than thirty years. Allison had done courses on cake decorating and made the most amazing sponges and cupcakes. Her cakes always sold out at school fêtes. So I thought there must be a way we could make the most of our passion for good home-made cakes by selling them to friends and family.'

One morning, as Liz and Allison were sitting having coffee, they came up with a plan to make and sell cupcakes. They invested £150 each to buy ingredients, boxes and packaging, and started baking. 'Initially we thought we would sell our cakes to coffee shops and cafés. We thought if we could get a regular order for a hundred cupcakes a week it would be great. But businesses wanted such a high discount it wasn't worth our while. So we concentrated on doing everything privately.' With an offer from a web design student to build their website for £100, Dotty Cupcakes was up and running. 'Our first customers were mostly friends and family, but once we got our website going we started getting orders and were making a profit within two to three months.'

Early on, the mums attended a free business course, where they were given advice and ideas on how to promote their cakes. They also needed to take out public liability insurance for unforeseen circumstances, such as if a customer was made ill by one of cakes.

At first, the bakers got their cakes noticed by taking stalls at food festivals around Cardiff. 'For two years we had a stall at the International Food Festival in Cardiff. But our success was determined by the number of people there and the weather. If the weather was bad we would be left with lots of cakes. One year we did a Christmas fair at the Wales Millennium Centre, Cardiff Bay. The first weekend was brilliant. Our stall opened at 10 a.m. on the Saturday morning and by 11.30 Allison had sold out. I had to rush down with all the cakes we had made for the

Sunday, then go home and bake more. We were up all night baking and by the end of the weekend we had sold around eight hundred cakes. It was fantastic but was also a lot of work. The following weekend we were prepared and had baked another eight hundred cakes. Unfortunately, the fair wasn't as busy so we were left with lots of cakes. We ended up giving them away.

'The festivals were good for getting our name out to customers and advertising our cakes, but when the cost of having a stall at the International Food Festival went up to £500, it was too expensive for a small business like ours to afford. Also the cost of ingredients started to go up and we could not expect customers to pay more than £1.50 for a cake, so we decided to stop and concentrate on private orders, weddings and conferences. But a lot of customers we picked up at the fairs stayed with us.'

Over the years Liz and Allison have specialised in wedding cupcake arrangements on tiered stands instead of traditional fruit cakes. Business customers have included Barclaycard, Principality Building Society, Admiral Insurance, the Lord Mayor of Cardiff,

Marriott Hotels, BBC Sport Relief, and luxury candle shop owner Jo Malone. They also make cakes for graduation balls and birthday parties, instead of more traditional birthday cakes.

'If it was our sole business we would never survive,' Liz warns. 'We don't really account for our time. For us it's nice to get the extra cash but we wouldn't be able to survive on our profits. But for what we wanted it's been fantastic. We can make money doing something we enjoy and make a profit. But if we had to charge for our time, we would have to look at ways of being more cost-effective and going out and really selling ourselves.'

Liz and Allison's top tip

Check out sites like eBay and etsy.com for selling your crafts. Even if you are just a 'hobby' business person, you will still need to tell the tax inspector and expect to pay tax on your profits.

Chapter Eight

DO YOUR RESEARCH TO BE A SUCCESS

It's a sad fact that one out of five new businesses stops trading within the first year, and half within the first three years. The most common mistake is a simple lack of good research and planning.

But don't let that scare you.

Rugby player Jonathan Hooper did his research and found there was a gap in the market for early-morning and day-time fitness classes in the area where he lived. So he set up his own – Hoops Health and Fitness Centre.

He was working part-time in his local leisure centre in Tonyrefail, where he was running two evening boxercise classes a week and supervising Sunday sessions in the gym. But he could see that by opening at 9 a.m. the centre was missing an opportunity to catch professional fitness fans at the start of the day before they went to work. 'When travelling to other countries, I saw different approaches to fitness, and felt that the leisure centre was missing out by not being able to offer that type of class,' he says. 'I would always go for a run or a work-out early morning before going to work and knew there were other people who did the same.'

Before he started working part-time at the leisure centre, Jonathan had been a regular gym user there since the age of fourteen. At school he was captain of his school rugby team and spent much of his spare time keeping fit. As an adult he played rugby for semi-professional club Caerphilly and the Welsh Rugby Sevens team, while working full-time in the customer services department at Natwest Bank. But after six years in work Jonathan got the chance to turn his love of sport and keeping in shape into a career. The bank was closing the Cardiff centre where he worked and Jonathan, faced with redundancy, decided to go back into education. As part of the redundancy package the bank helped him with this, so he went to study Applied Sport Science as a mature student at the University of Glamorgan. After leaving university with a first-class degree Jonathan considered being a Physical Education teacher, but was unable to get a place on the highly competitive training course in Cardiff. 'I did get offered a job working as a freelance personal trainer in a Cardiff chain of gyms but having just graduated I didn't have the confidence and business acumen to work for myself, so I found a temporary job in the customer services department of the Royal Mint.'

Temporary turned into permanent and in the next four years Jonathan worked his way up to database analyst. With his fitness background he was also responsible for providing inductions at the staff gym. When the gym manager at his local leisure centre wanted someone to run some fitness classes, Jonathan took the chance to step in. 'I enjoyed working in the leisure centre as it was what I had trained to do, but over time I started feeling frustrated. I could see that there was a customer base that had fallen off and they needed something fresh and new to get them back in through the doors. I wanted to offer more variety of classes and at different times. I convinced the managers to let me try a new fitball class, using exercise balls, and I was also allowed to launch classes at 10.30 a.m. to pull in mothers whose children were at school. But little changes like that took so long to convince the managers that they would work, that I felt there was more I could do on my own.'

Finally, in January 2010, Jonathan decided it was time for a fresh start. After two years of market research and weighing up the risks involved, he gave up his job at the Royal Mint and spent his savings on an intensive 12-week course to retrain as a personal trainer, with the aim of launching his own fitness training business.

'I completed the course one Friday, and the following Monday I launched my first outdoor circuit training class in the park behind the leisure centre where I worked. I advertised it among my friends on Facebook and at 6 a.m. I drove over to the park with my kit bag and waited for customers. Twelve people turned up. We ran laps around the park and did different exercises, and it all took off from there. All through the summer I ran classes on Monday, Wednesdays and Fridays. As that got more popular I hired local community halls and started running evening classes in boxercise. I wanted to introduce kettle bell weight classes into the area and I had asked the leisure centre but they didn't have the money and simply wouldn't buy the equipment. So I spent £800 of my own money buying enough bells to start a new class. It was a bit of a risk, considering I was working for myself. I would park my van outside the community hall half an hour before the class and unload all the weights from the back, then carry them all in and set them up in the hall. At the end of the night I would take them away again. That was my work-out!'

Over the following months Jonathan built up a reliable following for his classes, attracting an average of 10–15 people, mostly women, for each session, plus a few private personal training clients. In the run-up to summer the numbers would double with people – mostly women – wanting to get into shape for their holidays. But he was restricted in the times he could run classes as the hall was being used by other groups. Then he discovered an empty unit up for rent on an industrial estate in Tonyrefail.

'Speaking to my clients, I thought it would be nice to have a base so I wouldn't have to carry the kit around. And sometimes people would turn up at the wrong venue, so it would solve that problem. When I took out the lease on the unit it was an empty shell of a building. I spent a couple of weekends painting the walls and floor. Looking back I should have asked some of the rugby boys to help, but I was too independent. For the first year Hoops Health and Fitness Centre was really basic, with a concrete floor and a few mats, which was all I needed to run the kettle bells and boxercise classes. I wasn't aware of any start-up funding that might have been available to me, so I started off gradually. The following year I spent money on carpeting the gym and buying eleven spin bikes so I could introduce spin classes, which were popular in other places. It was a risk, but it added variety to the type of classes I could offer. Looking at the trends in countries like America the gyms at the forefront are more functional-fitness based.

'When I first opened in 2011, business was slow. A friend helped me to get a website up and running and most of my customers have come from word of mouth.

'The main difference to leisure centre training is that my gym is based around classes and is results-based training. People have fun but train with a purpose. I run at least seven or eight classes a day, seven days a week. And customers know when they come here there is someone to take them through a work-out rather than just going through the motions. I

used to get annoyed when I saw people in other gyms walking on treadmills or sitting on exercise bikes and reading a magazine. I felt that they were going through the motions rather than having a real work-out. In other gyms people go in to look good and leave without breaking into a sweat. In my gym no one cares what you look like. You come in to do your bit, and there are people there to help motivate you to work out. It's supportive, productive, training.

'Although I set out to work for myself as a personal trainer, working and living in Tonyrefail I found there wasn't the demand for that service as much as there was for classes, so that's the way I've developed the business. I still have a number of personal training clients around Cardiff and the Vale that I train at their homes. I am always aware of the number of gym members I have every month and I am proactive in trying new things to bring in new customers and keep existing customers motivated.

'Everyone knows the busiest time for fitness centres is January, after those new year resolutions, and also April, when people start looking ahead to summer, and sometimes also

September, after the summer. But there are quiet times of the year too, particularly in October to December, when casual customers drop off. So I realised I needed to introduce new classes There are ways of bringing new people into the centre and stimulating their enthusiasm to keep fit. I have the attitude that if things ain't working, let's make them work.'

Jonathan's top tip

Take advantage of the financial benefits for new start-ups.

Chapter Nine

WHERE CAN I GET MONEY
TO START MY BUSINESS?

No matter how small your business idea is, anyone planning to work for themselves will need some money when they start out, even if it's just to buy equipment or a van. If you are planning to rent a shop, office or workshop, you'll have to take into account ongoing monthly expenses such as rent, heating, lighting, phone bills and supplies. One of the main reasons businesses fail is that they don't realise how much the day-to-day running cost will be and how much money they will need to make every month just to break even. It may all sound scary, but if you have your own home and family, you're already doing this without thinking when you manage your household bills.

In 2010, Builth Wells pest controller Layla Bennett was given a £50,000 investment in her company by self-made millionaire Duncan

Bannatyne, when she appeared on the TV programme *Dragon's Den*. But it hadn't always been so easy for Layla to find money for her Hawksdrift Falconry business.

'Originally everything was done on a shoestring,' explains Layla, who set up Hawksdrift Falconry in 2006, while juggling a part-time job as a waitress and barmaid. 'The only money I had was my minimum wage from bar work. I never had money to save. If someone had given me £20,000 to start up my business I would probably be £20,000 in debt now. Back then I didn't know what was a good idea and what was a waste of money. It was better to learn slowly. It's surprising what you can manage without, when you don't have the money to waste. You have to come up with ideas that don't cost money.'

Layla was sixteen when she left home, dropped out of school and started working as a waitress. Growing up in rural Builth Wells, she had always been fascinated by birds of prey. As a young child she would try to spot red kites, which were then on the brink of extinction, She was also captivated by a sparrow hawk, which would often come down and prey on the smaller birds at her garden bird table. So when she found part-time work with a local falconer, she took the chance to learn the craft of caring for birds of prey. She discovered how effective birds of prey were in controlling colonies of gulls. Gulls would nest on the roofs of the steel work sites in Baglan and Llanwern, causing problems with maintenance of buildings and attacking workers. By flying hawks over the premises, Layla realised that falconers and their birds were able to scare the problem birds away. It was a natural and effective form of pest control. A year later she bought her first bird – a Harris hawk which she named Flame, and for the next five years continued to develop her skills in a field that was dominated by older men.

After several years working for other falconers, Layla decided to set up on her own, starting small. 'All I needed to start up was a van and reasonable clothes. I saved up and bought an old Citroen Berlingo for £2,700 from an auction. I thought it was a lot of money. I was living in a caravan in a field with no water and electricity, but my clients didn't need to know that. All they saw was me and my van and my hawks.'

At first Layla found it difficult to convince major businesses her falconry skills were the answer to their pest problems. 'These businessmen would see a young girl and didn't take me seriously. So a lot of my early work was at shows and carnivals, where I would take my birds and give flying demonstrations. I would also offer experience days where I would charge people to fly the birds. I was still working on minimum wage in bars. But I had friends who ran holiday cottages on their farm, Nannerth Farm near Rhayader, and I would advertise falconry flying experiences to their visitors. The idea really took off. Holidaymakers came to the cottages expecting the added attraction of flying falcons. At other times I would take my customers up to the farm to fly the falcons, and they would see the cottages and come back and stay there. No money changed hands. My friends were happy to let me use their land and I was happy to show clients their cottages.'

When an opportunity arose to buy an eight-acre plot of land for £45,000, Layla thought it would be a future investment where she could build aviaries. But she had no money. Layla says: 'I went to a bank and asked for a loan. But I needed a deposit of £4,000 of my own money, which I didn't have. I did have a credit card with a £4,000 limit. So I deposited £4,000 from the credit card to my bank account, which went against all sensible business advice. I was paying a high rate of interest on that £4,000 loan. It was a good couple of years before I paid it off. But I always just managed to make the minimum payments, confident that things would get better one day.

'Starting out I wasn't commercially aware at all. I just made it up as I went along. I had no formal business training so it was just sheer determination. I said to myself, "I want those contracts so I'm going to go and ask." I approached various businesses and told them I could do the job better or cheaper than others. Once I secured my first couple of customers, I was so keen to do it well that I provided a service that was far above what people were expecting and word of mouth spread.'

Gradually Layla's business took off and she started winning contracts from her rivals, and was able to expand to other areas.

Three years later, Layla entered the Powys Business Awards competition, where she was named Young Entrepreneur of the Year. 'That was one of the most amazing things to happen. Throughout my life people had said that falconry was not a good business idea and that

I should get a proper job. No one thought I would make any money from it. Even when they were trying to be helpful they were discouraging me. But for the first time ever proper business people, who knew what they were talking about, said that what I was doing was a good idea and I was a good business person. It gave me a huge amount of confidence. No longer was I just the "barmaid who kept birds of prey".'

Now that she owned some land, Layla also applied for start-up funding from Powys County Council, which gave her £2,500 towards the cost of building her first shed. 'The year after I won the business award Hawksdrift Falconry made £38,000, which I thought was good for a 25-year-old self-made entrepreneur who had started out with no money.'

Then one day, while Layla was sitting in her caravan, with her favourite hawk perched on her arm, her phone rang. It was someone from the BBC inviting her to appear on the programme *Dragon's Den*. A few weeks later, Layla and another of her hawks, Monty, were standing in the Den, in front of the panel of Dragons, which included Deborah Meaden, Peter Jones and Duncan Bannatyne. They were offering her £50,000 to help her build new aviaries and spend money advertising. Accepting Duncan Bannatyne's money, Layla spent the next three years expanding her business to take on four members of staff and increase the number of birds to thirty-eight, including Harris hawks, peregrine falcons and owls.

When the contract with 'Dragon' Duncan ended in 2013, Hawksdrift repaid the investment. 'At the end of the day it was a business investment and he was happy with the return on his money. We had certainly had a lot of work from it, mostly through the publicity, but we also had a lot of goodwill from Duncan. In the final year of our contract with him we turned over £200,000 and most of that came from commercial bird control. The only down-side of being on *Dragon's Den* was that I talked about our wedding ring delivery service. I hired out birds of prey to fly down the church aisle carrying the rings for couples getting married. Once the idea was featured on television there was no way of protecting it and other businesses starting competing. But it was a small price to pay for the publicity we got. I still offer experience days, wedding ring delivery and falconry displays but it's only a small percentage of my turnover.

'I was hard on myself to start with as I thought I wasn't good enough, but over the years my confidence as a businesswoman has improved. However, when I turn up on a job with a new client taking one of my male staff, the client always assumes that my employee runs the company. There's nothing I can do about that. Pest control and falconry is very male dominated. Being young and female I often come up against "What does she know about hawks?" But because I use less traditional methods and spend time with my birds, the birds are happier. They are no longer nervous of humans. My favourite bird, Hope, is like a dog; he spends all his time with me and has no fear. I have picked up a lot of contracts from businesses where falconers have said that they can't fly a bird because it's too noisy or because there are fork-lift trucks operating in the area which scare their birds. So I take Hope out and demonstrate that he will ride happily on the back of a fork-lift truck. He's been brought up to believe nothing will hurt him. I can use him in any environment.

'I believe my business sense has developed as I have needed it to. If you lose money when you have little to start off with you learn a hard lesson very quickly. You learn never to waste money and look for new ways of making money. I still live in a caravan but I now have running water and I've had planning permission to build a dwelling on the land next to my aviaries. So the future for Hawksdrift Falconry is exciting.'

Layla's top tip

If you can afford one thing – pay for a good accountant to keep on top of your tax bills.

Chapter Ten

WHAT'S IN A NAME?

Quite a lot, actually. Choosing the right name for your business can be fun. There are lots of businesses around which have silly names. Surely you've seen a hairdressing shop named Curl Up and Dye? Or what about a wine shop called Planet of the Grapes or a flower shop named Florist Gump? Some of my favourite funnies are The Found Sock laundrette and the pet-sitters who call themselves Hairy Pop-Ins.

But naming your business is also a serious step. There's a saying that first impressions count. That's why you should take time and get it right. Your name will tell people what your business stands for.

When choosing a name, ask yourself: does it tell people what you do?

If you live in the Cardiff area you may have laughed to see a learner driver having a lesson with a driving school called Bumps. To older drivers the name may conjure up visions of accidents and dented bumpers. But for the target market of teenagers it's proved popular. When the owner Keith Willicombe first came up with the name he wanted something that was different. 'I didn't just want to call it Keith's School of Motoring like other driving schools,' he says. 'I thought of fairgrounds and bumper cars. I considered calling my school Bumpers with the cars painted like dodgem cars. But I thought maybe driving test examiners would think I wasn't taking it seriously and would mark my students down. But the name Bumps stuck in my head. When I mentioned the name to my dad, he said, "No one's going to want to have lessons with a driving school called Bumps." However, Keith's instinct was proved right.

'When I picked up my first car from the signwriters with my new logo on it, I drove through the centre of Cardiff and people were pointing and laughing. They will remember the name, I thought to myself. And they did. The majority of my pupils are teenagers and the name appeals to them. Most new customers come to my school because they've seen the cars on the road and remember the name. So being different was a gamble, but it has worked.'

Once you have decided on a name, check that it is not the same or very similar to someone else's trademark. There are lots of stories of people who have fallen foul of this one. One example is Cardiff corner shop owner Nasser Afghrani, or Naz as he was known to his customers. Naz thought it would be funny to call his tiny corner shop NASDA with the sign painted in bright green, bold letters. However, the supermarket giant Asda threatened to take him to court over the use of its trademarked name.

Even if you're planning to use your own name, check out other people with the same name. You don't want to find out that you share a name with a famous porn star. Imagine the shock your customers could get when they Google you!

Chapter Eleven

LEARN SOMETHING NEW

There may be times when you have a plan, but don't have everything it takes. For some, that may be simply learning about the basics of running their business, but for others it may be retraining for an entirely different line of work.

A good example of this is father-of-two Kevin Arnold, who now runs his own therapy business, Momentum Coaching, from his home in Llantwit Major. Kevin had never considered working for himself. For over thirty years he was employed by British Telecom. However, due to various changes work had become stressful and when the company was looking for people to take redundancy, Kevin volunteered.

'Even though it was my decision to leave, I was tentative,' Kevin explains. 'After working somewhere for over thirty years I had become set in my work routine. It was a giant step into the unknown. I was fifty-one, divorced and my daughter was thirteen, my son was eleven. Even though I had left my job with a redundancy payment equivalent to a year's pay, I had a mortgage to pay on the family home, so I needed to find another job quickly. Looking back, it was a brave decision as I was walking away from a well-paid job. It would have been easy to become trapped in another job, where I had a decent income but was unhappy.'

For the first time in three decades, Kevin signed on at the Jobcentre and started applying for vacancies. 'I applied for jobs in schools, and in a photographer's studio. I even applied for work in a local estate agent's office. But most of the time I didn't even get a reply.' During a visit to his local Careers Wales office, Kevin discovered the Welsh Assembly Government's ReAct (Redundancy Action Scheme) which paid grants to retrain people who had recently been made redundant. Sitting down with an advisor, Kevin considered some of the opportunities available and the things he was interested in.

'We were going through options and the advisor suggested retraining in some form of therapy. I thought that if I was going to learn something new, it would be easier if it was something that stimulated my mind. I had an interest in Neuro-linguistic Programming (NLP) therapy, which was taking off in America. It's similar to hypnotherapy but not as well known. In Britain many people hear about it through the work of Paul McKenna and his books. I had read lots of them, including the most famous *Change your life in Seven Days* which uses elements of NLP. I was fascinated by the way a person could be taught to reprogramme his or her mind to make positive changes. The more I thought about it and talked with friends, the more I thought I would focus on retraining as an NLP practitioner. If I could get the necessary qualification I could advertise for clients and bring in business of my own.'

Finding a course in south Wales, Kevin spent every weekend for the next two months training, and during the week he practised what he had learnt. After qualifying in 2011 he launched Momentum Coaching. 'I was able to claim a New Enterprise Allowance of £65 a week for the first three months and £33 a week for the following three months, so I had some money coming in while I was finding clients.' He was also paired with a business mentor from Prime Cymru, an organisation which helps the over 50s into work and self-employment, who gave him advice and support with pricing and advertising. To keep his costs down, a friend helped him set up his website and he used a room at his home for seeing clients.

'When I started out I did quite a few sessions for free to get my name out there. I knew what I was offering was quite unique – many people are not as aware of NLP as they would be of something like hypnotherapy. I offered various NLP techniques and coaching, working on the basis that the mind can be reprogrammed to make positive changes. Those changes can then be used to manage common issues such as stress at work, stopping smoking, losing weight, conquering shyness, building confidence and managing phobias. It can also be used as an effective way to relax. The work I have done so far has been richly rewarding in quality rather than quantity.

'I love the freedom of working for myself and being in control. I don't miss going out to work every day. I am happy in my own company, so self-employment suits me. It also means that I am there for my children when they are growing up and studying for their exams. When I left work I thought self-employment wasn't for me, but I was wrong.'

Kevin's top tip

Take advantage of all the free mentoring and retraining programmes available. Accept invitations to events where you can meet other people and promote your business.

Chapter Twelve

HAVE YOU GOT WHAT IT TAKES?

So you think you want to be your own boss. The big question is: have you got what it takes? Do you have the right personality? Unlike normal jobs, there is no perfect job description for an entrepreneur, but there are common qualities that make some people better suited than others. Things like determination, confidence, patience, positivity and creative thinking. But you also need to be open to new ideas, willing to take the lead at times and to listen to advice at other times. The ability to plan ahead and take risks is also high up on this personal 'job description'. If you don't have business skills, don't be deterred; they are easier to learn than personal skills. If you're not the most organised person – can you hire someone to help you? If you don't like talking about money, you can always ask a friend who does. But basically it all comes down to attitude.

'You can have the greatest product in the world but if you have the wrong attitude you will never get anywhere in business,' warns dyslexic cook Margaret Carter, who now runs one of Wales's leading food businesses, the Patchwork Traditional Food Company.

'In my business I have met lots of people who are passionate about the food they make, but they just don't know how to sell themselves, or their products. My advice to them is to employ someone who can. And you have to be likeable – no one wants to buy a service from someone they don't like, whether it's having a haircut or taking a car to a garage for a repair, so if you have a bad attitude – drop it.'

Margaret has been running her company in Llangollen for thirty-one years but admits she was terrified of taking those first steps to market her own home-made pâtés when she started out in 1982. 'I was always deemed to be stupid because of my dyslexia. I was not brought up to be a businesswoman. I came from a background where I believed I would get married and be taken care of,' Margaret explains. 'When I moved to Llangollen after my marriage broke down I had three children to look after, a mortgage to pay and I had to find a way to make money. I asked myself "What can I do to make money?" In the 1970s Margaret had run her own successful business in London making jewellery, then luxury jumpers which sold in the fashionable Kings Road and Harrods store. So she knew she had the drive and determination to work for herself. But the recession hit, people stopped spending money on luxury items, and Margaret had to close her business and moved to north Wales to be close to her family.

'Two of my children were working in a local restaurant, so I came up with the idea of making home-made jars of chutney. I asked the restaurant owner if I could sell them at his restaurant.'

Naming her jams 'Patchwork' after the piece of patchwork she used on the lids, Margaret soon found her jams weren't selling. So she asked the restaurant staff for advice. The chef suggested she should try making pâté. Margaret says: 'I had never heard of pâtés, and had no idea how to make them. But I went home, dug out some old cookery books and discovered that they were a type of French spread made with minced meat and herbs. That week I saved up £9 from my housekeeping to buy the ingredients and made my first batch of liver, brandy and herb pâté.

'Once I had made the pâtés, I found myself too scared to try to sell them! I had pinpointed five pubs and restaurants and deli shops in the area I thought might like to buy it. So I put the pâté in little plastic pots and drove off to visit the owners. But when I got to the first shop, I was afraid they would say no. I turned around, went home, put the pots back in the fridge. I told myself, "I'll do it tomorrow." The next day I did exactly the same. Finally on the third day I phoned my friend and said, "Will you be my driver? Don't take me home until I've got out of the car."

'Once I'd finally gone into the cafés and left samples, I went home and cried for ages. I was worried that they would hate it. I picked up the phone to call them, but put it down again. I couldn't face the rejection. I was afraid I would be told that the person who had eaten my pâté couldn't come to the phone because it had made them ill. When I finally gathered enough courage to call them back, they all said they loved it and placed regular orders. It turned out I had nothing to be scared of. Most people I know find it hard to push themselves, but if you don't you will never get anywhere, as I found out. If you need to get money you need to get up and make it happen, whether it's cleaning windows or making jam. There are plenty of things to do if you have to earn a living but you have to get off your butt and do it.'

Suddenly with five new customers, Margaret had to learn how to make larger batches. Gradually as word spread, more customers started to stock her products and in 1987 the Patchwork Traditional Food Company moved from her home to a factory in Ruthin. Over the years it has grown as a brand and now sells all over the world. They even supply airline company British Airways with pâté, which they serve to first-class customers on their flights.'

Today, the Patchwork Traditional Food Company employs thirty people. Its pâtés have won almost eighty awards and Margaret has been named Welsh Woman of the Year. Yet the company still remains true to its home-made values, everything being hand-made in small batches using Margaret's original recipes. 'I am still driven to be the best,' says Margaret, who is a Dynamo Role Model for the Welsh Government's Youth Enterprise campaign and visits schools, colleges and universities inspiring young people. She says, 'The attitude "that will do" is not an option for my business. If you are starting your own business, whether you're making jam or building a house, you have to set out to be the best you possibly can. If you are making a product and customers like it, then don't mess with a successful formula. The chicken liver, brandy and herb pâté we make today tastes identical to the one I first made, because that's what people want to buy and that's the way to be successful and be in business for thirty years. People won't buy it if you change the recipe. Once I visited a food fair and there was a stall selling cakes. I bought some chocolate brownies and they were delicious. When I went back the next day, the stall holder sold me some but told me, "They're not so good today. I burnt them." If that had been my business I would have put them in the bin and started again, I certainly would not have sold them.'

Margaret's top tip

Always get better – never go backwards.

Chapter Thirteen

ARE YOU READY FOR HARD WORK?

Being your own boss is not the dream job many people imagine. If you get it right there are bonuses but it can also be a lonely, demanding and uncertain journey.

'If you're in business you don't have one boss, you have many bosses. Every one of your clients is your boss. To succeed you have to do a good job and keep them all happy,' says Glynn Pegler, founder of digital strategy and content producers Culture Group.

'Anyone who thinks the idea of running your own business is an easy ride should ask themselves what they mean by hard work. I went six years without a holiday and made a lot of sacrifices along the way. If you run your own business, you can't leave your desk at 5 p.m. and go home. If something needs to be done urgently the buck stops with you. You have to make sure it gets done. It takes a while to adjust and accept that. For a lot of clients there is no room for error. People demand perfection and my job is to do my best to deliver that. Once I had no sleep for five days in order to meet the deadline.'

Culture Group is a business with its headquarters in Cardiff Bay and employs the services of some twenty people who work with clients like Google, Red Bull and Virgin Group. Glynn, the founder and Chief Executive, has been his own boss for fifteen years and he's just turned thirty!

Glynn first noticed he had a head for business as an eight-year-old in primary school in Rudry, near Caerphilly. 'I was the kid in the corner of the yard flogging my wares. I used to make cakes and Christmas decorations at home and sell them. I would keep enough money to cover my costs and give my profits to the school.'

By the time he moved to comprehensive school in Caerphilly, Glynn had started to become disillusioned with careers advice. 'I was terrible at maths but I always enjoyed design and art. I wanted to be a magazine journalist but one of my English teachers told me I would never make it. My level of English and grammar wasn't good enough.' But an art teacher spotted Glynn's flair for design and suggested he get involved in the school magazine. Two editions later, Glynn was editor, at the age of fifteen. 'I approached a local radio station and set up an interview with the DJs, which I wrote about in the magazine. Then I thought: if I can produce a magazine for my school, why not for schools in the whole borough of Caerphilly, or even south Wales? I brought together a group of friends and got support from our local council to distribute the magazines. Then I approached the Prince's Trust charity, which gave us an award of £10,000, which we used to buy computer equipment, rent offices down the road from the school and pay to print the first couple of issues. I quickly learnt how to design magazines using desktop publishing software and how to get the magazine ready for printing. I was sixteen when we launched our first magazine at Caerphilly Castle. It was given out to schools and at public venues across south Wales. I think everyone was expecting a photocopied rag. They were very surprised to see a glossy magazine, backed by celebrities.' Aimed at young people, the magazine featured advice about health care and careers and interviews with major stars like Beyoncé and Usher.

For three years Glynn ran *Culture Magazine* which came out every two months. Then one of the directors of the charity NCH (now known as Action for Children) called Glynn and asked if the magazine would be able to run a campaign to find out why young people were not interested in mainstream politics. 'I thought to myself "Do you realise you are talking to a teenager?" I had no experience of politics but I thought I'd give it a go!' The result was one of the UK's first main text-messaging campaigns called Text Tony. Young people were encouraged to text their views on laws, the government, and the Prime Minister of the time, Tony Blair, to a mobile number. That number was just a spare phone that Glynn had in his office. At that time social media was new, Facebook and Twitter hadn't been invented, and mobile phones were still only used for calls and text messages. The campaign made the news and soon Glynn and his team found themselves at the Labour Party conference standing next to the Prime Minster himself and American president Bill Clinton.

Glynn realised he was on to something. 'I saw how I could run similar campaigns with other brands. So I started looking at what else we could do. I liaised with the Prince's Trust who were creating a market place at the Glastonbury Festival and went along. The first year, I found myself backstage taking photographs, which were used around the world to market the official TV coverage of the festival. The following year I went back with a team of eight people and within five years we were a team of some 120 people working on the festival co-ordinating all digital content and website workings. The work received over a billion hits.

'It got me thinking: how can I build a company and do these things to create a positive impact for other people? As a result Culture Group's strength has been in creating strategies and digital content that drives marketing campaigns to create positive social change. Over the years they have worked on campaigns for clients including Google, Red Bull, Virgin Group, Comic Relief and social enterprise backers UnLtd. In 2013 Glynn was appointed a UK ambassador to the European Cultural Parliament's youth network. He also co-founded a social enterprise called Young Brits, which works with young entrepreneurs. In 2013 Culture Group set up its first international office in Mexico.

'I used to have to hide my age as I found it difficult to be taken seriously. Competence, not age, should be what everyone gets judged by and the fact that I was a teenager shouldn't have mattered but it did. Over the years my confidence developed and the experience I've gained now allows me to support other young talent from all over the world.'

Glynn's top tip

Keep up to date with new trends and advances in technology.

Chapter Fourteen

WHAT HAPPENS NEXT?

You've read the stories and now you're fired up with your own ideas of how you can work for yourself. So what's next? Sometimes it can be stressful finding the support and resources you need to start out and the money to pay for them, but there's no need to be alone. In Wales there is a wealth of free business advice and support available to people starting out on the road to self-employment. Here are just a few of the many places you can turn to for help.

The Welsh Government's **Business Wales** provides business support to people starting, running and growing a business. Their website has all the detailed information you'll need to get started. They also have advisors on the end of a phone and business centres across Wales. Their phone helpline is open between 8 a.m. and 6 p.m. Monday to Friday (except public holidays). **Phone** 03000 603000
Website www.business.wales.gov.uk

If you're aged between eighteen and thirty, and are unemployed or working less than sixteen hours a week, **Prince's Trust Cymru** offers an Enterprise programme giving young people advice as to whether their business ideas will work or if self-employment is right for you. They have courses running at centres all over Wales and every year they help hundreds of young people to start out on their own. You can sign up for a short information session followed by a four-day Explore Enterprise course to learn about topics relevant to planning and running a business. You can learn how to manage money, market your business, and understand finances and cash flow. They'll teach you the difference between turnover and profit. (Turnover is the money your business makes each year, profit is what's left after all your tax and other bills have been paid.) And at the end of the course you'll be paired up with a mentor, who is an experienced business person who will help you put together a plan for your business to make sure it's a viable option. They'll send you off to test the market, finding out if people want to buy your product or service, and with your plan in place they will help you apply for grants and loans of up to £4,000 if you need them. And once your business is up and running the Prince's Trust mentors provide regular support during the important first two years.

Phone 0800 842842 or 029 2043 1500
Website www.princes-trust.org.uk

For over 50s, there's **Prime Cymru** (The Prince's Initiative for Mature Enterprise in Wales). The registered charity was set up by Prince Charles in 2001 in response to letters he had received from many older people saying that they felt they were on the 'scrap heap' after the age of fifty, and found it hard to find work because of their age. There are over 210,000 people aged fifty to state pension age who are not working, many through no fault of their own, and Prime Cymru's staff and volunteer mentors, some of whom lead successful businesses across Wales, are helping them with support and confidence-building to start out on their own. Over the years 1800 people in Wales have achieved their dream of working for themselves, thanks to Prime Cymru.

Phone 0800 587 4085
Website www.primecymru.co.uk

Business in Focus has been helping people start their own ventures for almost three decades. They have offices dotted around Cardiff, Swansea and the valleys, where teams of advisors are skilled in helping new businesses. They run a series of free half-day courses where you can learn the basics of business from starting out, researching your market, finding and keeping customers, setting your prices and managing your finances. They can give you all the help you need to stay on the right side of the law and keep the tax inspector happy. They also offer one-to-one mentoring once your business is up and running and have office space and factory units available to rent. Almost nine out of ten businesses starting out on their courses succeed.
Phone 0870 950 90 90
Website www.businessinfocus.co.uk

Big Ideas Wales is a Welsh Government Campaign to inspire young entrepreneurs under the age of twenty-five. They have a group of people called Dynamo Role Models, who help to motivate and stimulate enterprise in young people. Check out their website for advice on schemes and funding for youth enterprise.
Website http://ms.fs4b.wales.gov.uk

If you're unemployed, **New Enterprise Allowance** can provide money and support to help you start your own business if you're getting certain benefits. It offers start-up loans and a weekly allowance totalling up to £1,274 paid over 26 weeks.

Website https://www.gov.uk/new-enterprise-allowance